Untangled
The Journal

Matador
Unit E2 Airfield Business Park,
Harrison Road, Market Harborough,
Leicestershire. LE16 7UL
Tel: 0116 2792299
Email: books@troubador.co.uk
Web: www.troubador.co.uk/matador
Twitter: @matadorbooks

ISBN 978 1805141 839

British Library Cataloguing in Publication Data.
A catalogue record for this book is available from the British Library.

Printed and bound by CPI Group (UK) Ltd, Croydon, CR0 4YY
Typeset in 11pt Adelle Condensed by Bhavini Lakhani.

Matador is an imprint of Troubador Publishing Ltd

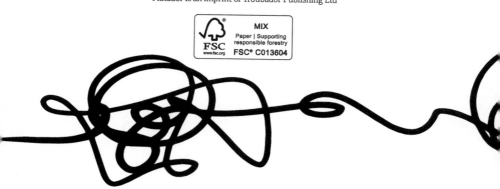

For my daughter Scarlet,
with endless love.

If found, please return to

....
....
....

Contents

> You are your own
> home base.

Untangled

Untangled Journal

Introduction

You may have chosen to create change, you may not. And yet here you are, picking up the knotted cords and gently teasing them apart so that your future can become a reality. It takes courage. It's not easy. It is absolutely worth it. Take a minute to just reflect on the fact that you are in this, and you are being intentional about the life you are living. That's a gift to yourself and it's a gift to those around you. The more you show up and live your life authentically and with courage, the more you inspire and support others to do the same. So from me to you, thank you. Keep going.

This book can be your place to reflect on the change you're living through. Taking your thoughts and feelings out of your head and heart, and onto paper, allows you to step back, look at them, and choose what you do next.

I wrote Untangled to bring together the skills, tools and resources we need for change we've chosen and change we haven't. This Journal is designed to be used alongside that book. It's a beautiful place to hold your thoughts. And it can be used by itself if you just want journal prompts to support self-reflection.

So congratulations for saying "yes" to being more intentional about the way you live through change. For many of you this might be the first step in discovering who you are and who you are becoming.

Kirsty

How to use this journal

I'll start by saying if you're a 'quick start' person then here's your permission to get stuck straight in! There's no way to get this wrong, so go for it. If you're more someone who likes to do a deep dive, then I really recommend having a copy of Untangled alongside you as you use this journal - it's the source of all the content here and has way more in terms of inspiration, stories, examples and support for you as you work through change.

Let it be a living breathing place to hold your thinking and pondering.

Carry this journal with you as you work through change. I've deliberately made it big enough to write in but small enough to be portable! If you're going to the office, take it with you and scribble some thoughts on your commute. When you're out and about at the weekend, make time to sit down for ten minutes with a cup of coffee and give yourself the gift of some journalling time. Head out for a walk, sit under a tree and ponder for a while. Having the journal won't do the work for you, but it can certainly help! The only thing you need to do next is start to write, let the words fall from your pen and see what emerges. It can be amazing how much you can discover simply by sitting for ten minutes and asking yourself a simple question.

Give yourself permission to be creative!

Some of my most useful journals have been the ones where I've allowed myself to be fully creative - I've used coloured pens, stuck in poems or quotes that I've found or printed out, made lists, used stickers, added photographs and really made them my own. I can't even draw a circle, but adding colour and outside materials captures my imagination, feels liberating and inspiring!

Use the writing prompts to suit you

Take the journalling prompts as launchpads and see where they take you. If a prompt doesn't work for you or feels limiting, take it in a different direction. With coaching clients I always say there are no wrong answers, and I never know where the questions will lead. Some may bring pages of reflection, others a sentence or even one word. It's all okay.

Notice where you want or need support

Going through change is not something to be done alone. Pay attention to where you need or want support and choose who you want to support you. That might be a friend or family member, or it might be someone with professional training in how to help you through change. Suitably accredited coaches and therapists can bring deep skills and further tools to help you. To find out more visit www.untangledbook.com where I explain the difference and help you find someone who can support you through change.

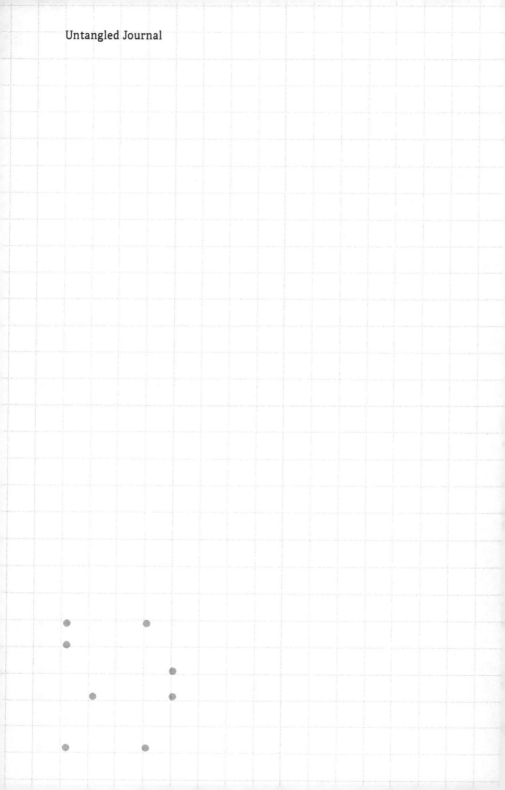

Pieces of my story

I've lived through many different types of change in my life, and I've helped thousands of others to do the same - as individuals, teams and even whole organisations. I know it can be some of the most challenging things in our life. My own life has seen me choose and create incredible changes, from the smallest changes like deciding to stop colouring my hair, through to designing a home and creating a business. I've also been forced into change that life has thrown at me, shaken and thrust into situations I never would have chosen, including job loss, divorce and bereavement.

I've ridden the waves of change, even at points when I thought they might drown me. I've sat in those moments of completely not knowing which way to move forward or how to keep going. What I know for certain is that we will always face change, and we can discover ways of living through it. We can develop things that help us to feel more resourced and better equipped to make choices and be intentional about how we move through it. It isn't always easy, it is always worth it.

Untangled has much more of my story. For here I simply wanted to share that I see you, I know this can be tough, and I'm here to remind you that you are not alone in facing change. Even the change we choose can be incredibly challenging and it can also help us to live a more fulfilling life, with increased satisfaction and a renewed sense of purpose.

My wish is that Untangled and this Untangled journal bring you increased clarity, a sense of support and newfound ways forward. I'd love to hear from you about what your biggest insights are and any pieces where you're still uncertain. You can always message me through www.untangledbook.com to share your story and questions.

PART 1

UNTANGLING THE MYTHS

Chapter 1 of Untangled shares the myths of change and busts through them so they don't hold you back. It shares my own story of coming to realise that these myths were getting in my way. Here they are as a summary for you to reflect on.

Myth: You have to take a giant leap
Reality: You can take baby steps or crawl if you have to

Myth: You need self-belief
Reality: Self-belief is waiting on the other side of the change

Myth: You have to have complete clarity
Reality: You can start with what you already know

Myth: You need to get less sleep
Reality: Sleep is vital

Myth: You have to be single-minded
Reality: You can be multi-minded and still find focus

Myth: It's either you or them
Reality: It's you with them

Myth: You can drop all the other balls
Reality: You can drop the rubber balls, they'll bounce

Myth: Change has to look good
Reality: Change doesn't look good in the messy middle

Myth: You have to drive change
Reality: Change will drive you; cling on

Myth: You have to be kind to yourself
Reality: You do have to be kind to yourself - It just might look different from what you've been told

Which of the myths is hardest for you to let go?

What would be possible if you could put that myth to one side?

Reality 1: What's the first baby step you could take?

Reality 2: What would you dream of if you totally backed yourself?

Reality 3: What do you already know about what you want
to create?

Reality 4: When is a good time of day for you to prioritise your future?

Reality 5: What else are you responsible for?

Reality 6: Who's in your world?

"We are wired to have hope and to stay with things that don't serve us, in the belief that things will get better. We never have complete certainty, we always have doubts. The future isn't guaranteed to be better and we can step into it regardless."

Untangled

Reality 7: What are the balls you're juggling? Which ones would bounce?

Reality 8: In what ways do you still believe change has to look good?

Reality 9: What direction is the change taking you in?

Reality 10: What are the ways in which you're not kind to yourself, yet?

Untangling the Change Myths Summary

What feels important to capture about the myths and the realities of change?

What insight and awareness is here for you now?

PART 2

UNTANGLING YOUR PATH

Clarify

The first step to untangle your path is to Clarify three things:

- who you are,
- what matters to you, and
- what you're good at.

Chapter 2 of Untangled gives examples and stories from my own life and my clients.

Use these pages to reflect on the wonderful human being you are - messy, imperfect and still fabulous (even when you don't feel like it!)

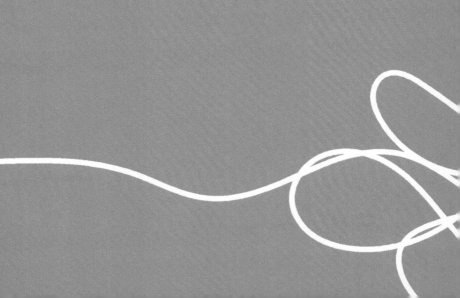

Who are you?

I am a person who...

At my core I ...

I want you to know that...

What's your purpose?

Use this story spine to start to capture your story - or at least one version of it.

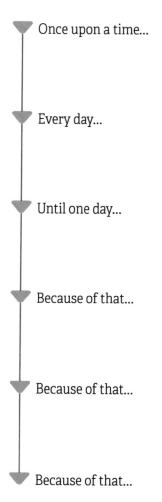

Once upon a time...

Every day...

Until one day...

Because of that...

Because of that...

Because of that...

(You can use this phrase as many times as you need to!)

And the moral of the story is...

What do you notice about your life so far?

What's the moral been?

Why have you been here until now?

Self belief is waiting
on the other side of
the change.

Untangled

What do you stand for?

What's your mission for this change?

What do you stand for?

What would you write on a massive banner if you were on horseback and wanting people to follow you up the hill? You can even draw it here if you like!

This mission will guide you throughout change. When you waiver or things get difficult come back to this page.

What are you good at?

What might become possible if you claimed your potential and your accomplishments?

What are you good at in your job?

What are you good at as a parent if you have children?

What makes you a good friend?

What are you good at, at home?

What are you good at in your community or as a citizen?

What are you good at in taking care of yourself?

What are you good at in your family?

What's your hidden talent that nobody knows about?

What would your best friend say are your strengths? (If you don't know, now is a good time to ask them!)

What's one thing that people consistently say you're good at? (This might be your superpower by the way!)

What energises you?

Revisit the strengths lists.
Mark with a star what energises
you and mark with a 'minus' sign
the things that drain you.

Do you notice any patterns
or themes?

Are there things you might need
to do less of, even though you're
good at them?

The Clarifying Threads

What's surprised you about this first step of Clarifying?

Are you surprised by how much you know or how much you feel is still unanswered?

How does that feel?

What's the piece you want to explore further just now?

What's the piece that still feels too hard?

What's the permission you need to give yourself to help you keep moving?

I give myself permission to.......

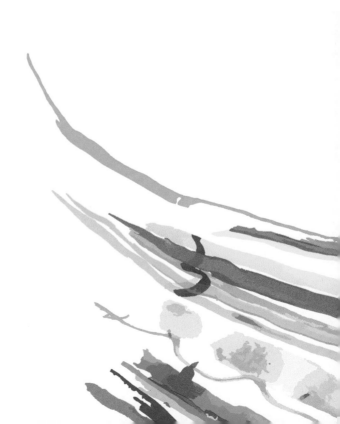

Clarify Summary

Use this two page spread to pull together the threads that you've untangled so far. You might want to add in photographs or doodles, or poems that have sparked some thinking. The more colour and energy you can bring to the pages the better!

I am

My purpose is...

My mission for this change is...

My core strengths are:

I'm energised by...

Connect

Connecting with ourselves and our lives gives us access to more insight to inform our actions.

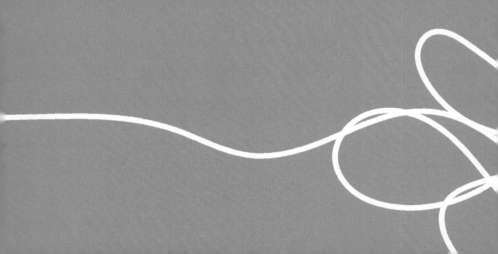

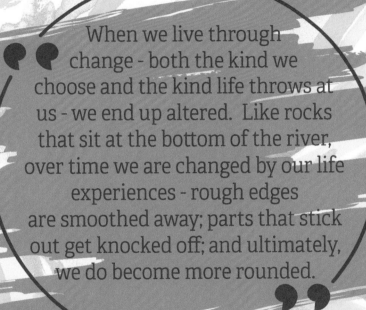

When we live through change - both the kind we choose and the kind life throws at us - we end up altered. Like rocks that sit at the bottom of the river, over time we are changed by our life experiences - rough edges are smoothed away; parts that stick out get knocked off; and ultimately, we do become more rounded.

Untangled

What's here now?

Take note of who you are now - maybe stick a photo of you in this book with a date on it, or write a few words about who you are now.

What's your starting point?

Who are you now?

What brings you joy and fulfilment in your life now?

What are you longing for?

Who do you want to become?

What do you appreciate about yourself now?

What's the story so far?

Use these next pages to reflect on the story of you and your life so far, looking at themes and patterns. You might want to use photographs from key times in your life. Perhaps you could print a map out and stick it in showing where you've been at key times in your life. Or even sketch some of the significant things in your life.

What's your story so far?

57

What relationships have been significant?

What have been your most memorable moments?

What was significant about them?

What does that show you about yourself?

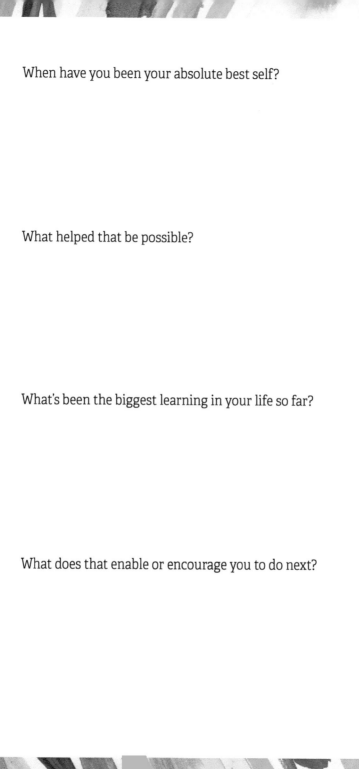

When have you been your absolute best self?

What helped that be possible?

What's been the biggest learning in your life so far?

What does that enable or encourage you to do next?

How do you feel and what do you need?

How are you feeling and what do you need?

Track your feelings and needs every day for a week and see what you notice. Set a reminder on your phone to help you remember. Page 195 has a list of emotions if you struggle to pin down exactly how you're feeling.

Day	How I'm feeling	What I need

What's getting in the way?

Let's identify the barriers that might get in the way of change in your life.

I'm holding back because...

If I go ahead with this change people will think....

I'm scared that...

My worst nightmare would be...

What do you notice about the things that are getting in the way?

How might a change of perspective help you? Let's identify new beliefs that you might want to try on and see how they shift things:

I am...

I can...

I will...

The Connect Threads

You're pulling apart the threads that were tangled so that you can start to weave something new. Let's look at them now:

What have the positive threads in your life been so far?

What are some of the current themes?

If your life was a movie, what would have been the story to now and what's the current act?

What might the soundtrack be?

What's most important to you right now?

Choose

Once we've clarified what matters to us and connected to who we are and what's important in our life, we can make the choices to guide us forward.

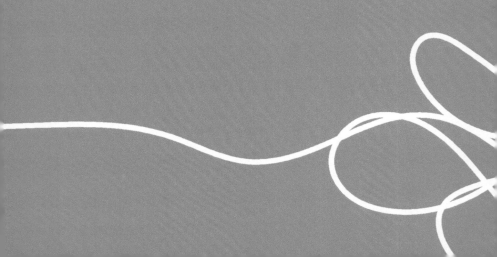

> It takes courage to listen to your inner wisdom, the part of you that still dares to dream, the part of you that wants to make a different future.

Untangled

What do you want?

Use each of these as prompts to write for 60 seconds non-stop. Set a timer and let's go! You might want to write each answer on a separate card like I suggest in the book Untangled. Then you can capture the most important thoughts here for future reference.

What do you want twenty years from now?

What do you want ten years from now?

What do you want five years from now?

What do you want a year from now?

What do you want six months from now?

What do you want that's just for you?

What do you want for your family and those you love?

What do you want for your community?

What do you want for your country?

What do you want for humanity?

What do you want to have?

What do you want to do?

What do you want to be?

You might want to write these things on the Venn diagram and look at where some of the crossovers are.

Where does this fit into your life?

What's the story you want to be able to tell about this time of change?

What do you want to feel most proud of?

What challenges do you want to have overcome?

How could the change alter your priorities for the better?

What's the ideal?

Use this wheel of life to reflect on how fulfilled you feel about different aspects of your life. You can label the segments in any way that works for you. Possible categories include physical wellbeing, work, family, leisure, spirituality, romantic relationship, community, wealth but you can use them however works best for you. Search online for wheel of life if you need more ideas or visit www.untangledbook.com for examples. You can even use this to look at particular aspects of your job and evaluate how satisfied you feel and where you want to make changes.

If you're feeling totally fulfilled, colour in that section of the wheel fully (ten out of ten). If you're not feeling at all fulfilled, maybe leave it white or colour in only one or two out of ten.

For each section, you might then want to reflect on the following questions:

- What would make it a ten?
- What needs to change?
- What's the place I want to start?

You might find this quite daunting, so give yourself permission to start with one section where you feel you want to create a change. You don't have to do it all overnight!

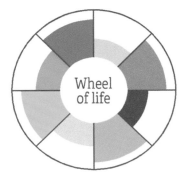

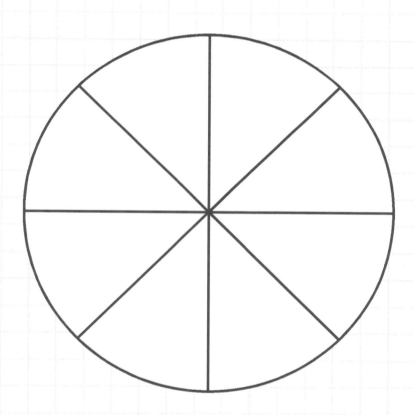

I first came across the wheel of life as a coaching tool through my training with CTI www.coactive.com

Untangled Journal

What's important about the change?

Why is it important to you?

What's the core of this change?

Who are you going to become through this?

What's the nature of this evolution of you?

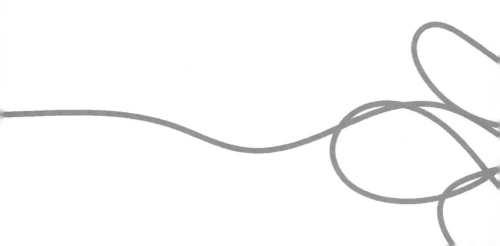

Who's on your support team?

Write the names or initials of those who are in your support team. These are the people who've got your back. They will cheer you on when things go well and commiserate when things don't go well. It's sometimes also helpful to have someone who is slightly distanced from family and friends, like a mentor, a coach or a therapist.

Choose Summary

What's the change you want or need to make in your life?

What's the bigger picture for that change that feels significant now?

What themes in your life is this change related to?

What happens if you don't evolve?

What's the adaptation worth to you?

Human beings are a curious mix.
On the one hand, we are wired
towards evolution. We need to
keep changing. On the other hand,
we like the status quo and are
predisposed towards homeostasis.
We gravitate towards stability.

Untangled

PART 3

UNTANGLING YOUR WAY

How to handle your feelings

Living through change brings a whole raft of different feelings - it's normal. We are not our feelings, they will pass. And there are things you can try to help you with them in the meantime.

When change feels constant

Sometimes change feels like it's never-ending. We live through one thing after another without any space to draw breath.

Success Strategy:

Make a little space for yourself.

What could space look like? Is it physical space or mental space? Inside or outside? Small moments more regularly, or bigger chunks of time once in a while?

What do you need to be able to stop the dizziness and find some inner stillness?

Who in your support team can help you with this?

When change feels negative

Change can feel negative - we know what we don't want.

Success Strategy:

Paint the bigger picture of what you do want.

What's the thing that you really want to have, do or be?

What matters to you?

What's your dream?

When change feels false or fake

We can occasionally wake up and realise that the change we're focussed on is not the real change. The dream we've been pursuing is fake.

Success Strategy:

Reconnect with your values.

What do you really want?

Repeat the question to yourself at least five times

If nobody ever knew, would you still want it?

Are you doing this for yourself or to try and gain approval from people whose opinions don't even matter?

When change feels impossible

If you're feeling trapped, stuck or completely without options, the change around you might feel impossible.

Success Strategy:

Start with the step closest to you, the one you don't want to take.

What's the closest step to you right now, that will move you towards the change you're creating?

What's the one step you don't want to take?

What will help you to take that first step?

Who can support you?

What does taking it even more slowly look like?

When change feels premature

We can get ahead of ourselves in facing change and try to dive in too deep, too soon.

Success Strategy:

Pause. Forbid yourself to make any changes for a fixed amount of time.

Take time to really reflect on who you are and what matters to you.

What is really important?

What if it took you ten years to achieve?

What's the root desire in this?

When change feels circular or zigzag

Sometimes it feels like change follows anything but a straight line and the destination feels out of reach.

Success Strategy:

Prioritise your destination and stay open to the magic along the way.

Write down all the aspects of the change facing you, one thing per piece of paper. Then work through each pair and choose the one that matters the most. Keep repeating that 'sifting' until you have the top 10 things that really matter to you. Full instructions for this activity are in Chapter 5 of Untangled.

What truly matters to you about this change?

(And yes, some of these questions are repeated, because the more clarity we have about what truly matters, the more alignment there can be in how we live our lives)

When change feels imposed

There are times when change feels imposed and there are times when change is imposed. Many of us struggle with the feeling of being out of control.

Success Strategy:

Identify what's within your control versus what you can influence.

In the smaller, inner circle, draw or write the things you can control.

In the larger, outer circle, draw or write the things that you can influence.

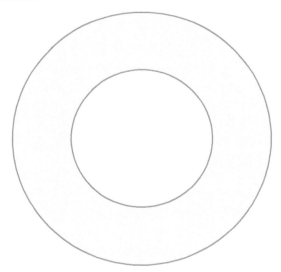

Use this to remind you that you are never totally powerless, you can always have choice over some aspects of change.

How to Handle Your Feelings Summary

When change feels...

When Change Feels	Try This...
Constant	Make space for yourself
	Revisit self-care
Negative	Paint the picture of what you do want
	Revisit your bigger picture
Fake	Reconnect with your values
	Journal on what you really want
Impossible	Start close in with the step you don't want to take
	Go slower than a slow thing
Premature	Pause
	Forbid yourself to change
Circular or zigzag	Prioritise your destination
	Stay open to the magic
Imposed	Identify what you can control
	Identify what you can influence

How to Ride the Waves of Change

Change brings with it successes and failures, highs and lows, releasing and embracing.

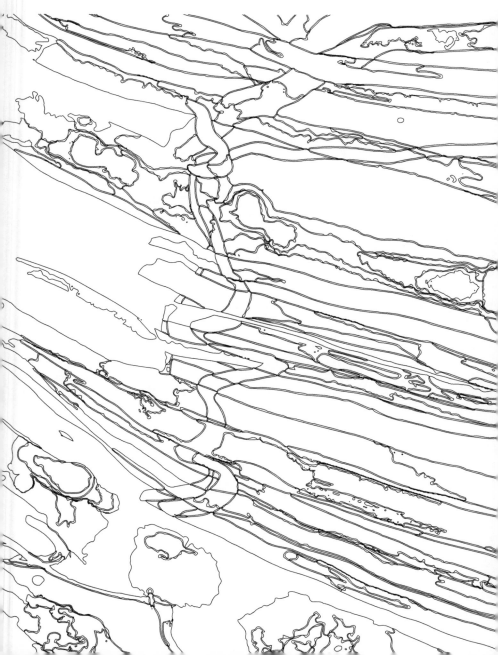

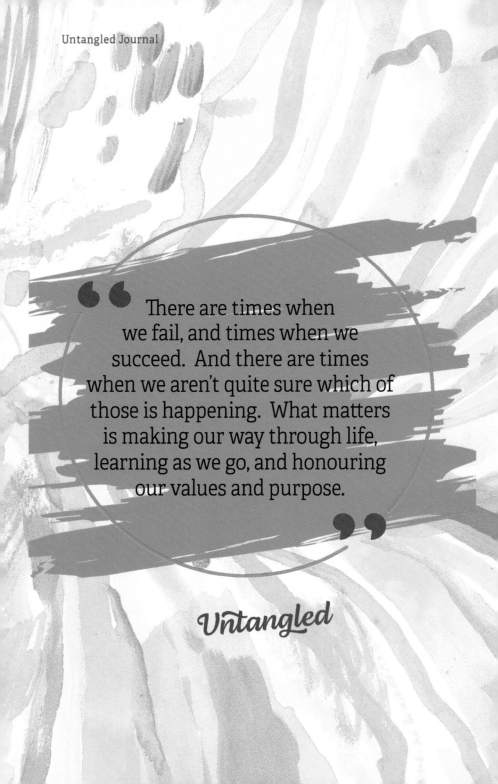

"There are times when we fail, and times when we succeed. And there are times when we aren't quite sure which of those is happening. What matters is making our way through life, learning as we go, and honouring our values and purpose."

Untangled

Why letting go is hard

We do not find it easy to let go. We cling on. To jobs, relationships, old habits, even physical possessions. We are wired to have hope and to stay with things that don't serve us, in the belief that things will get better.

We never have complete certainty, we always have doubts. The future isn't guaranteed to be better and we can step into it regardless.

Where are you clinging on and you know you need to let go?

What's keeping you from taking the first step?

How to identify what no longer serves you

We start by recognising what's not working for you right now. You may be able to create changes and improve things, just by identifying what's not working in your current context.

Thinking about the change you're facing at the moment, complete these sentences:

I can't cope with...

I get frustrated with...

It would drive me crazy if....   lasted forever

I feel compromised when...

I'm ready to change...

I want more...

I want less...

You can write as many responses as you want to for these and then see what themes emerge.

What are you ready to let go of?

How to let go of the old

Once you recognise what you need to let go of, it's time to actually let it go - even when it feels difficult. Sometimes physical ways of releasing can help us process the emotions of endings.

Five ideas of ways to let go

- Write it out on paper and burn it

- Write it on paper and bury it

- Write it on pebbles (in eco-friendly pen or pencil) and throw it into a lake or pond

- Write it on toilet paper and flush it down the toilet!

- Write the words in the sand and let the sea take them away

What's going to help you feel more free?

How will you let go?

How to handle it when it doesn't work out like you hoped

Sometimes things don't go according to plan. We can never predict what will happen. Sometimes the biggest, boldest, most beautiful hopes we have for our future end up smashed on the rocks. Here are some steps to take when things don't go the way you thought they would:

Step 1: Pause

Step 2: Look at what has worked

Step 3: Reconnect with what matters

Step 4: Redesign what needs to be different

Step 5: Start again

Untangled Journal

Your space for thoughts and reflections

Why failing at something doesn't make you a failure

If something happens and I believe that I have failed at it, I'm going to pick myself up, dust myself down and try again.

If something happens and I believe that I am a failure, I'm much more likely to give up, hide under the nearest rock or in my bed, and not come back out again. Or at least not want to.

We can get caught up believing that our very being is defined by our results.

When we are already feeling raw from dealing with reactive change, any sense of failure can hit us even harder. Self-compassion and self-care matter so much when we're going through change we didn't choose. At times it makes me want to scream, but it's true.

You are not a failure, even when you fail spectacularly.

What does failure mean to you?

What would your life be like if you'd never failed?

What's a helpful belief for you to hold about failure?

How to pick yourself back up

You've fallen flat on your face (metaphorically) and failed spectacularly - or even just a little bit. How do you get back up again?

▼ Step 1:

Recognise that you've fallen flat on your face and get curious about how you're feeling.

- How am I feeling?
- How did I get into this situation?

▼ Step 2

Notice what stories you're making up. Pause long enough to notice what stories you're telling yourself.

- What's the story I'm telling myself about the part I've played?
- What am I making up about the part that others have played?

▼ Step 3

Recognise what patterns there are in your thoughts and actions. This is where the learning lies and the chance to write a new way forward for yourself.

- Which of these thoughts and beliefs are new and which are old patterns?
- What do I want to choose about this situation?
- What's the story that helps me to grow and move forward from here?

(Adapted from Rising Strong by Brené Brown and Dare to Lead™)

How to learn from your failures

Don't even try to learn from your failures straight away. When you fail, and you get yourself back up again, you can't learn the lessons straight away; give yourself time.

Once some time has passed - a few hours or days for small failures and setbacks, weeks or months for the bigger ones - take time to reflect.

What did you experience?
- what happened (without interpretation or analysis)

What did you learn (or relearn)?
- be as specific as you can

How will you apply the learning?

Riding the Waves of Change Summary

Use this page to gather together your key reflections on riding the waves of change

What no longer serves you?

How will you let go of the old?

How will you handle it when it doesn't work out?

What's your trick to picking yourself back up?

What's the learning from your failures so far?

Your ability to ride the waves of change just increased exponentially!

Celebrating You & Your Successes

Whether you've been working through change you've chosen or change life's thrown at you, it matters that you take time out to recognise and celebrate who you are and what you've achieved - even if that's getting out of bed in the morning when you just want to hide away from the world.

Sometimes we find it almost impossible to recognise what we're achieving and our focus is more on what we're *not* doing.

What do you find easy to recognise and celebrate?

What feels more difficult?

When was the last time you did something to celebrate you, who you are and what you've achieved? Have you celebrated other people more recently?

What stops you from celebrating you more often?

"

Celebrating seems to make the results last longer and it means we are able to learn from what we've achieved as well as from the things that haven't gone as well.

"

Untangled

How to recognise what you've accomplished and who you've become

Take a few slow breaths and start to pay attention to who you are right now. Allow yourself to recognise who you are in this moment. Everything you've accomplished and achieved in your life so far. Take it all in. You could even look in the mirror as you do this and really acknowledge the amazing person in front of you.

You might find this is difficult or impossible. I share stories in Untangled of clients where this has been some of the hardest personal development work they've ever done. So be gentle with yourself and if you need help ask a friend or reach out to my team to see how working with a coach could help you at www.untangledbook.com

Take time to start a list of what you're good at.

I am good at...

I find it easy to...

People ask me to...

I'm known for...

I've always been able to...

Pay attention to the 'what' and the 'how'. Maybe you've moved house, so the 'what' is moved house. The 'how' is all the things it took to get there, for example, thinking of where you wanted to move to, clearing out old things you didn't need, being brave and telling your children, organising the finances, saying thank you to your old neighbours etc.

What skills have you demonstrated?

What qualities of yours shone through?

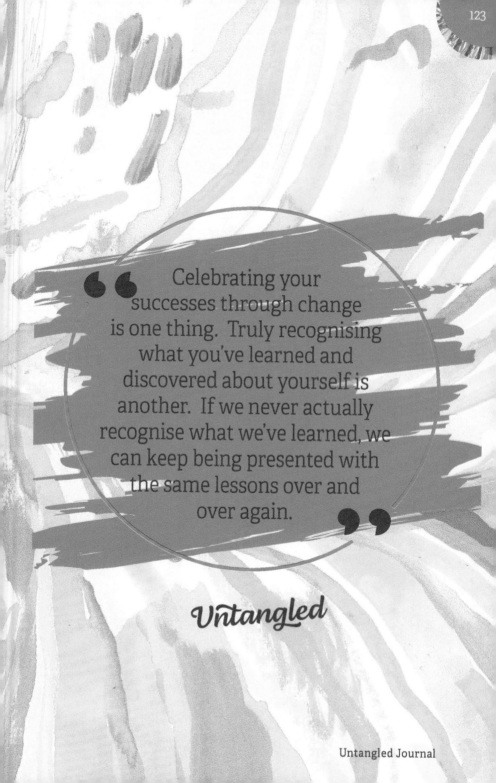

" Celebrating your successes through change is one thing. Truly recognising what you've learned and discovered about yourself is another. If we never actually recognise what we've learned, we can keep being presented with the same lessons over and over again. "

Untangled

How to capture what you have learned through change

It's time to reflect on the insight and wisdom you have about yourself now as a result of recent change. If you're still in the middle of change, bookmark this page and come back to it in the future. You can do these as short prompts or take longer over each one - whichever feels more helpful for you now,

What have I learned about myself?

What have I re-learned about myself?

What was my biggest discovery?

What surprised me?

Who have I become through this?

Which part of me is growing the most?

What have I been able to let go of?

Where am I still holding onto something that doesn't serve me?

Where have I gained the greatest support?

What's been my biggest challenge?

Sometimes in writing these things down it can feel important to share them. You might want to share them with a close friend or family member, or to work with a coach so that you can take that insight even deeper.

How to discover what's possible for you now

Once we recognise what we've learned and what's here now, we can start to look at what's possible for us next. Think of it like climbing a spiral staircase, we might look at the same things with a different perspective.

Even through change we've not chosen, we learn from it anyway. I learned so much about myself from losing my mum, although it's a change I would have done anything possible to stop. Looking at what's possible is where the learning and insight opens out into new opportunities.

Set a timer for three minutes for each of the following prompts and let your thinking reveal itself. There may be some repetition or themes that emerge.

I can now...

I believe that I...

I know that...

I am ready to...

I want to...

It's my time to...

What's here for me now is...

From the outside I now seem more...

From the outside I now seem less...

The biggest possibility for me now is...

How knowing your love language can help you celebrate in your style

Which of the following matters to you the most?

It's most meaningful to me when someone I love:

- Gives me a hug (love language = touch)
- Gives me a small and thoughtful present (love language = gift giving)
- Spends time with me (love language = quality time)
- Sends me a note saying what they admire about me (love language = words of affirmation)
- Does something practical to help me out (love language = random acts of kindness)

What else lets you know you are valued?

There are 15 ideas of ways to celebrate in Untangled. What's important is choosing a way to celebrate that feels valuable to you. Remember it can also be the smallest of things, you don't have to put money into celebrating, it's the intentionality and thought that you put in which will make it the most meaningful.

What ways of celebrating really make you feel special?

What's a way you'd love to celebrate?

How do you celebrate others?

What's the way you choose to celebrate who's here now?

Celebrating You and Your Successes Summary

This has been a big chapter and might have pushed you to thinking about when, where and most importantly, how you celebrate success. Gather these threads into their new current shape here.

What things that you've accomplished have surprised you most?

What's been your most significant learning?

What's the most expansive thing that's possible for you now?

What insight has reflecting on love languages given you in how you choose to celebrate?

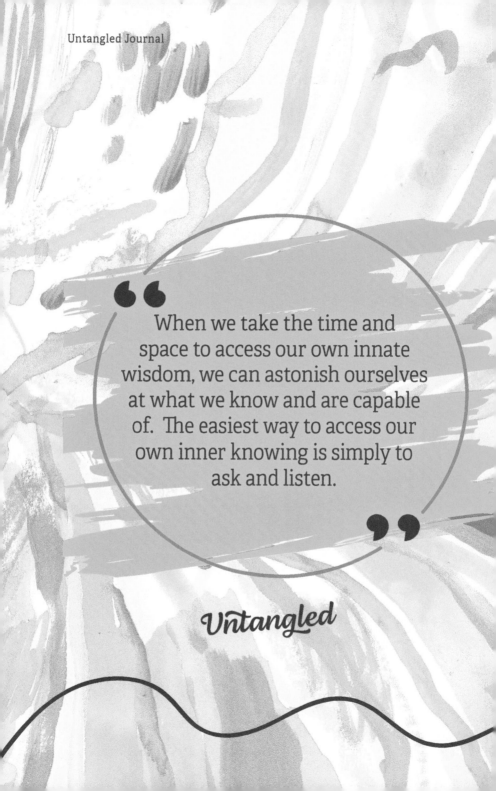

" When we take the time and space to access our own innate wisdom, we can astonish ourselves at what we know and are capable of. The easiest way to access our own inner knowing is simply to ask and listen. "

Untangled

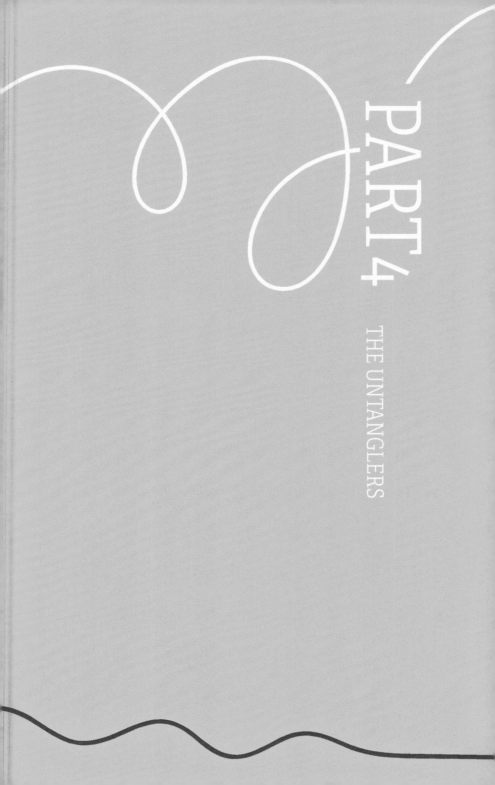

PART 4

THE UNTANGLERS

Overcoming barriers to change

Different barriers we face will take different strategies to overcome them. Being equipped with those strategies before you need them will help you keep moving and make it less likely that you'll get stuck for longer than necessary.

When you hit a barrier, you need to recommit to the overall aim of your change and that helps you to know you are on the right track. Remember that there are people who can help you with this - you don't have to go it alone.

How to handle fear

"I'm scared. Bad things are likely to happen."

Sometimes we stall because we're scared. We set out with good intentions and somewhere along the way we are reminded of the future uncertainty and we stop. Frozen to the spot by the knowledge of what's unknown. It's natural and it doesn't have to keep you in that spot forever.

The success strategy is to face your fear - and ask for help if you need it. It sounds scary, it is possible and in Untangled I share more stories of how I've faced fear head on. It can help to have someone to help you face it, a coach or mentor who can acknowledge that it is scary and help you to keep going.

What are you scared of?

What if that wasn't true?

What becomes possible if you face that fear?

Who can help you to face your fear?

How to handle shame

"I'm not good enough. I don't deserve to be happy."

Shame is the most painful of barriers, because it's the sense that you are not good enough. That snarling voice in your head that stops you from living the life you are truly here to live. It's enough to stop us as we move through change and it often drives disconnection as we try to hide our perceived failings from other people.

The strategy to overcome shame is to do what's counter-intuitive at the time and reach out to others, call your friends and tell them how you're feeling. I guarantee they'll know that feeling and be able to support you. Putting it into words reduces the power shame has over you.

What are your strengths and best qualities? (Look back at the previous sections to what you've already written)

What if you are already good enough?

Who's your best source of support when you feel that you're not good enough?

Write the initials of three friends you can call when you're gripped by not feeling good enough.

"I don't know what I want."

Sometimes we realise that we don't actually know what we want or where we're going. Perhaps you never really identified it in the first place. Maybe the initial goal was a false goal or false destination, the real goal sits behind what we initially see.

The strategy is to revisit your overall purpose and mission and get clear on what really matters to you.

What is it you don't know, when you say "I don't know what I want"?

What does clarity give you?

What if you did know what you wanted?

What if you dared to believe that what you want is possible and you deserve it?

How to overcome inertia

"I can't be bothered."

I think of this as the "can't be bothered" barrier. This barrier will try and convince you that the changes you are facing no longer matter. Sometimes this is a cover for other barriers that are deeper, but most of the time it's a stalling tactic that our minds use to keep us from really living a fulfilling life.

The way to overcome inertia is to take small steps, to move closer to the desired destination. Taking action, any action, is going to create momentum. Even setting a timer for five minutes and using that time to move forward will start to melt the inertia.

What's one thing you can do today to get moving?

What would you do to help a friend get started if they were in your shoes?

One year from now, what will you be proud of?

"I've got too much to do"

Being too busy is the number one reason for not getting where you want to get to. Everyone has the same twenty-four hours in the day, yes, even you. And yet, some people manage to achieve all kinds of things and others less so. If you're aiming for something and it doesn't ever happen because you never quite put it at the top of your priority list, it's time for you to reprioritise.

The strategy to actually start to prioritise what matters is to trust yourself and listen to what you really want. We have to start by getting really honest about whether or not we believe we deserve the change we're trying to create. If not, the real barrier is self-belief. If you do believe you deserve the change, then it's time to change your core beliefs about what it means to prioritise yourself. And that starts by taking action and including yourself on the list of priorities.

Which of the rubber balls do you need to drop? (See change myths at the start of this journal)

What's it worth to prioritise yourself?

Who can help you to put yourself higher up the list of priorities?

Barriers to change will occur. This section has helped you to identify the tools and strategies to mean they don't completely stop you in your tracks.

Here's a reminder of the strategies and space for you to make your own reminders.

Barrier	Reminder	Your notes
Fear	Face your fear	
Shame	Call your friends	
Confusion	Revisit your purpose	
Inertia	Move your ass!	
Lack of prioritisation	Trust yourself	

Discovering Change Skills

The chapter on change skills in Untangled takes you through guided activities for each of these skills. If you have the book you can use these pages to work through those and capture your thoughts and feelings. If you don't have the book you can use the journal prompts to kickstart your reflection and expand these further on the notes pages.

> Change skills are the kinds of skills that make you look like a ninja warrior when you use them in your everyday life. People will see you riding the waves of change that life throws at you, making bold moves as you launch yourself into new ventures and generally thriving.

Untangled

Finding your purpose

Purpose is the "for the sake of what" of our lives. What's the reason for you getting up in the morning? What's the life you want to live?

What's your purpose?

Why are you here?

Let yourself listen to the tiny whisper or the giant roar in your heart.

Notes on purpose

Honouring your values

Our core values guide us through tough choices, help us live with integrity and are often the reason we get wound up about the same things over and over again. When we live in alignment with our values, we tend to feel more fulfilled, and we find decision-making easier. But when we are out of synch with those guiding stars, things feel off-centre, unbalanced and it can be difficult to know what we want.

What are your top two or three values?

For each of them:

I know I'm in alignment with this value when I ...

I know I'm on the slippery slope out of alignment with this value when I ...

You can find a list of values as a starting point at www.untangledbook.com

Notes on values

Practising self-care

Self-care is a skill that comes with a serving of tough love because it's one that many of us struggle with. When change comes into our lives, our lack of ability to take care of ourselves can come at a huge cost. We all know of friends and colleagues who've been dealt cards of change, only for it to be the thing that broke them.

I also want to be clear I'm talking about deep self-care, beyond the superficial buying ourselves flowers or going for a long drive in the car. The self-care we need in change is the things we need to truly care for ourselves. Things like saying "no" or putting in place healthy boundaries.

Take care of you. Exquisite care of you. You are the one thing you can (learn to) count on.

Start to create a list of ways in which you can take care of yourself. Here are some starters for ten from Untangled:

- Ask a friend for suggestions
- Think about what someone you really admire might try to do
- What would you suggest to a child?
- What's the thing that could make the biggest difference?
- What's the thing you would be scared to do?
- What's the one thing that feels impossible but also super-helpful?
- What would you do if your life depended on it?
- What's the thing that feels so simple it almost feels silly?
- What would you do if you knew it was guaranteed to work?
- What's the one thing your heart and soul needs?

Notes on self-care

Living with self-compassion

Self-compassion and self-care are different, even though they may sound the same. Self-compassion is the way you talk to yourself in your head. Start to pay attention to the inner conversations you have with yourself and you might be surprised! We often say some pretty harsh things to ourselves and it can take work to notice that and start to act with more self-compassion. Untangled has more information on this and it's definitely an area where it can help to work with a professional coach (see www.untangledbook.com) or therapist. In Untangled I share how it helps me to think of these inner conversations as radio stations, the journal prompts are based on that idea.

To start with, notice what you say to yourself in your own mind and make notes on the following:

Which radio station are you listening to you in your mind?

What's the main soundtrack?

What prompts you to listen to one station over another?

How can you listen to a different radio station in your mind that might be more supportive?

What might that give you?

Notes on self-compassion

Becoming friends with vulnerability

Vulnerability is risk + uncertainty + emotional exposure (Dr Brené Brown). It's the feeling in your stomach when you don't know what's going to happen, but it doesn't feel like it's going to be good. It's when you want to run away, hide or sometimes come out fighting. It's a core part of facing change and it's not pleasant. It's another thing that can completely stop us in our tracks if we don't become aware of it and recognise that we can choose to keep going.

It helps to get specific about what's at the root of our vulnerability and then to do the thing that defies logic and reach out to someone else. Connecting with another human being might seem like madness, but it helps us to realise that we are not alone.

What feels most vulnerable?

What's the worst that could happen?

How likely is that?

What might happen instead?

Who's earned the right to hear your fears and help you to move forward?

Notes on vulnerability

Discovering your courage

You can't face change without courage, because facing any kind of change is scary. People often think that being courageous is the absence of fear. But it's not. It's seeing the fear and walking towards it, rather than turning and running the other way.

For the next seven days, notice the fear that comes up in your life. Make a list here of all the things that you're scared about, where fear is getting in the way.

Once you have made your list, stop and take a look at it. For each thing ask yourself the following questions and write about them.

- What if the story that I'm telling myself is just made up?
- What if the outcome was different and potentially more positive?

Then, reflect and journal on the following:

- What's the best thing that could possibly happen?
- Could it be that the step is worth taking after all?

Notes on courage

Discovering Change Skills Summary

I believe that change skills should be taught in schools. Since they haven't been yet, it's time for us all to start practising them. You won't build them all overnight, so pick the one that feels most useful for you for right now and start to put it into practice in the context of the change you're facing.

Make yourself a summary note on what you've just discovered:
Finding your purpose

Honouring your values

Practising self-care

Living with self-compassion

Becoming friends with vulnerability

Discovering your courage

Pause for just a minute or two and reflect on what becomes possible now that you have these things at your fingertips. It's quite a magical thought!

Using Change Tools

In Untangled I give step-by-step guides to each change tool, and stories of them being used in real life. If you have the book, these pages are yours to capture what you notice and experience in using those in your life. For those who don't have the book use these pages to write down your thoughts and feelings. Let this section become your own personal toolbox of things that you can return to, as you face change in the future!

These tools will help you to take action and create the changes that you want to see in your life and organisation. And for change that you're reacting to which has come from external factors, they can help you to adjust and focus on how you can move forward.

Making the vision tangible - creating a vision board

We are capable of creating pretty much anything we desire - if we can dream it, we can create it. And while you might not personally believe that, you just need to look around you for evidence that this is true of humanity. Every single thing that you can see in your current environment was once imagined by another human being, or it's a force of nature.

Create your own vision board and stick a photo of it here to help you get clear on what matters to you and stay connected with that as you move through change.

Here are some sample powerful questions, and you can also add your own.

What do I need to know now?

What's in my best interest today?

What's getting in my way?

What's the greatest gift I have now?

How am I sabotaging myself?

How can I be my greatest support?

Who am I today?

Where can I get support today?

What's the next step for me to take?

What can I do to take care of myself?

And here are more which you might want to reflect on over a period of several days or weeks and see what themes emerge. In coaching these are more enquiry-like questions. You're not expected to be able to answer them straight away - they invite deeper reflection.

What's my future?

Who am I becoming?

What's the role for this change in my life?

Where am I holding back?

What do I truly long for?

What's the core of this change?

What's the growth here?

Where can I let go?

What's next?

Notes on powerful questions

Getting to know your gremlins or your inner allies

Here we're getting to know the different parts of you and the different aspects of yourself. I was introduced to these as gremlins in my coach training. Since then I've learned more about different ways of thinking about ourselves. I now believe it can be more helpful to look at our internal dialogue as different aspects of ourselves that are trying to keep us safe.

In practical terms these are the voices in your mind that stop you from engaging with change. They'll tell you that it's safer, or better, or less risky to stay with the status quo.

It helps to get to know those voices and to notice the thoughts on a daily basis (it's one of the reasons we do so much journalling). Then start to look at the thoughts and ask yourself where they come from.

What's my thought?

Where does it come from?

Is it helping me to move forward or is it more fear-based?

Does it come from the grounded, centred, level-headed version of myself, or does it come more from a place of anxiety and protection?

How real is that fear?

What do you actually want and need?

If the fear wasn't there, what would you do?

If the thought comes more from a place of trying to keep yourself safe, ask yourself:

What do I need to feel safe-enough and still move forward?

I should probably have started the whole of Untangled and the whole of this journal with this section. Asking for help is a vital part of helping yourself to thrive through change. It's not always easy to ask for help, and we've mostly grown up learning not to do so. If you're facing change and have any other form of responsibilities, it's pretty much essential. The help you need might be small or large, the barrier to accessing it tiny or massive.

What help do you need?

Who might be able to help you?

Now reach out to them. Ask them now to help you and simply see what happens next.

My biggest tip for this is to keep breathing, and the next one is to keep your request for help as general as you can. You might be surprised what shows up.

Some examples of help you can ask for:

- Looking after your kids or pets for a bit because there is something you want to do (not just something you have to do)

- Helping you research something to do with your chosen change

- Baking you a cake because you need cheering up

- Spending an evening with you sorting out old photographs for a funeral you need to arrange

- Staying on the phone with you while you fall asleep because you don't want to be alone

- Sitting with you while you phone the doctor to make the appointment you don't want to make

- Going to the doctor or dentist with you

- Going shopping with you for clothes for a job interview

- Reviewing your business plans even when they are really sketchy, and you don't want anyone else to see them

- Working with you to set out your monthly budget or your current financial position, even when you feel like resisting it to the hilt

- Getting out for a walk with you because you know you need to start to exercise and it just all feels too hard

Your ideas

You can share your suggestions at www.untangledbook.com and help to give ideas to others facing change!

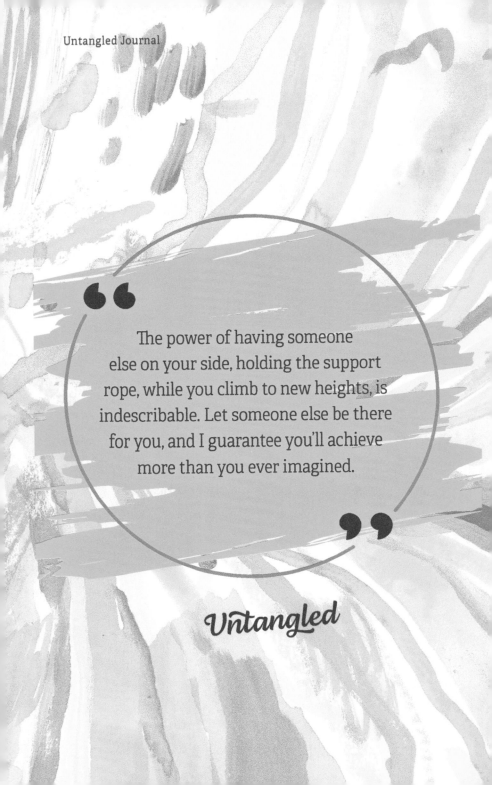

> " The power of having someone
> else on your side, holding the support
> rope, while you climb to new heights, is
> indescribable. Let someone else be there
> for you, and I guarantee you'll achieve
> more than you ever imagined. "

Untangled

There will be parts of any change - even change you really long for - that you just don't want to do. Or maybe you want to do it, but you're scared to, or think you can't do it, or just want to be on the other side of it. This is where accountability comes in - sharing what you're going to do with another human so that they can hold you to it. This might be a friend or a coach or someone in a peer coaching group.

What accountability do you need?

Who can help to hold you to account without any judgement?

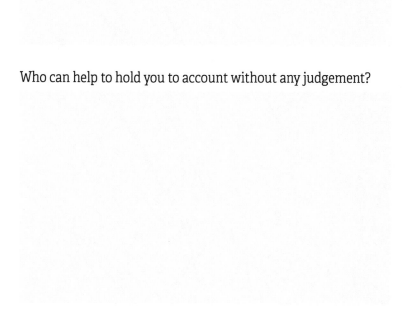

Four Questions for Accountability (for your friend or a coach to hold you to account)

- What will you do?

- By when?

- How will I know?

- How do you want me to be with you, if you don't follow through?

Gratitude - the antidote to guilt

Gratitude can be the antidote to the guilt we often feel, the sense that we've done something bad. This can often arise during change, particularly if we are focussing on ourselves and historically we believed that this made us selfish. Gratitude can be your salvation if you are afflicted by guilt like I have been at many points in my life. The trick is to make it an active practice, a thing that you do in a way that works for you, to stop and pay attention to what you're grateful for and express that gratitude.

Untangled has instructions on:

- Gratitude journalling
- Gratitude jars
- Gratitude photos

And

- Gratitude walks

Use this space to make your own notes about what you're grateful for and to commit to your own gratitude practices.

What are you grateful for?

What else are you grateful for?

What are you grateful for today?

What are you grateful for in this chapter of your life?

Who are you grateful for?

How might you express your gratitude?

Breathing and the dreaded "M" word

I've struggled for a long time with mindfulness, which is why I've called this section what I have. I wanted to include it because it's a really helpful resource to support you through change and Untangled gives a very tools-oriented view of it.

I share four techniques in Untangled:

- Mindful breathing
- Progressive body relaxation
- Counting breaths
- Tracing your hand

You'll find many more online. Start with what works for you, even if that means something that helps you to become aware of your thoughts for 60 seconds. Remember that the point of doing this is to increase your self-compassion and to reduce the impact of unhelpful chatter in your mind as you live though change. It's not to stop your thoughts!

What's your current belief about mindfulness?

Do you already practise mindfulness? If so, what helps you? If not, what gifts might it bring you?

What practice would you like to try for the next 30 days?

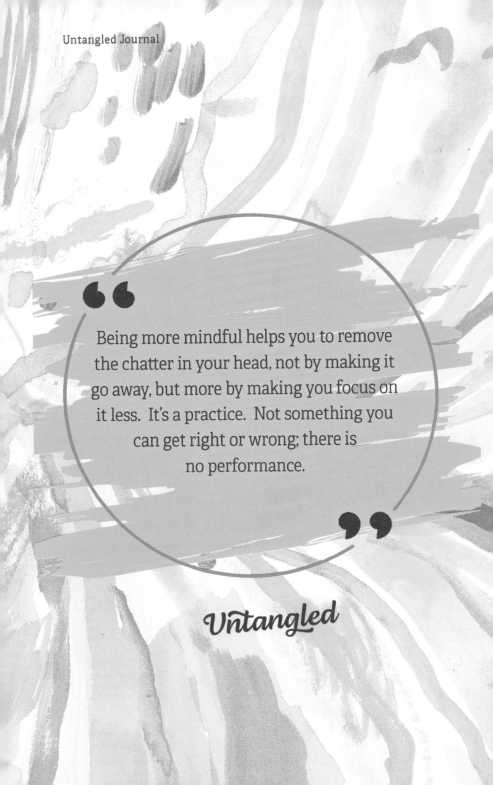

Being more mindful helps you to remove the chatter in your head, not by making it go away, but more by making you focus on it less. It's a practice. Not something you can get right or wrong; there is no performance.

Untangled

Feelings and needs

Change brings a lot of feelings with it, and if we don't pay attention to those feelings, they can end up running the show, through our behaviours. Paying attention to how we feel acts as a doorway to recognising what we need.

How do you feel?

You can use an emotions wheel to help you identify how you feel, it's a way of looking at the emotions that's visual and helps us to understand the relationships between them as well as getting more specific. Because it's quite detailed we have a download available at www.untangledbook.com that you might want to print out and put into the back of this book and we've included a list of emotions here. Noticing how you feel regularly will help you to expand your emotional literacy as well as connecting with your feelings. When we are able to recognise how we feel we have more choices about how to move forward.

Happy	Lethargic	Discouraged	Numb
Overwhelmed	Torn	Impatient	Worried
Ashamed	Fear	Hopeful	Depressed
Satisfied	Lonely	Surprised	Energetic
Curious	Neutral	Content	Angry
Anxious	Peaceful	Tender	Scared
Queasy	Grateful	Grumpy	Envious
Troubled	Puzzled	Irritated	Relieved
Stuck	Intrigued	Exhausted	Fulfilled
Amused	Annoyed	Excited	Disappointed
Tense	Calm	Vulnerable	Insecure
Reluctant	Hurt	Embarrassed	Bored
Comfortable	Indifferent	Inspired	Confused
Delighted	Frustrated	Pleased	Guarded
Enthusiastic	Furious	Encouraged	Stressed
Upset	Open	Tired	Unhappy
Amazed	Uncomfortable	Optimistic	Affectionate
Resentful	Disgusted	Shocked	Joyful

What do you need?

Slowing down to speed up

In the twenty-first century there are huge benefits to slowing down, it brings more awareness.

In Untangled I share two simple experiments you might want to try. Use the space here to reflect on what you noticed.

Experiment one - Slowing your walking pace

What did you notice?

What surprised you?

What difference might this experiment make?

Experiment two - Slow your shower

What did you notice?

What surprised you?

What difference might this experiment make?

Slowing down can actually bring us more speed. We can re-energise ourselves, become more aware of what we truly want and need, and gain new insight and clarity to inform the change we face.

Using Change Tools Summary

In this section you've done the work to develop your own set of change tools, strengthen your insight and increase your awareness. Whether you've dipped in and found the one tool you need for now, or worked through them all, they are here for you to return to. You might also have noticed that some could be useful for friends or family, so feel free to share them. The more you use these tools, the more powerful they become, so use this space to reflect on what you have access to now and how you might start to use them to support you in the coming weeks and months.

I now realise that...

I have discovered that...

I want to practise...

I am committed to...

I feel proud that...

Untangled Journal

A note from Kirsty

This book is now completely yours. Whether you've written a few words or many, whether you've worked through every section or just the ones you needed most, these are your words. Your thoughts and feelings, poured out onto the page so that you can work with them and make conscious choices as you move forward.

My greatest wish is that by working through this journal you feel more resourced to face change in your life - the kind you choose and the kind you don't.

I would love to know the thing that's been most helpful to you in this journal and any key pieces of insight you've gained. You can post your insight at www.untangledbook.com and inspire and help others who are also facing change.

Keep weaving your threads and know that you can return to these pages over and over again in the years to come.

Keep untangling.

Kirsty

Keep Untangling

This journal was always intended to be a companion to the Untangled book which gives much more rich content, stories and examples to inspire you along the way. I wanted to create something beautiful that you could use to work through the journalling prompts and capture your own words and images. If you don't already have the Untangled book it is available through all good book shops and directly from my publisher Troubador at www.troubador.co.uk

You can also access more resources, journal prompts and support through change by registering at www.untangledbook.com Here you can also register to receive new tools as I create them, and to be matched with a coach for one-to-one or group support.

If you'd like to work through change using Untangled in a book group, in your team or in your organisation you can download a Book Group Guide at the same website and we also offer group coaching programmes for organisations through The Firefly Group www.thefireflygroup.co.uk. The power of working through change in a group is immeasurable. We see that every day in our work with FTSE 100 and Fortune 500 organisations.

We're here to support you through change individually and in organisations, so do get in touch to find out more and let us know what support you need.

Acknowledgements

I want to take the space here to say how grateful I am for those who've helped me to get this journal into your hands. For my full acknowledgements of the wider work for both the book and the journal, see the words I've written in Untangled. Each expression of gratitude in those pages also translates to this journal.

Writing the book was a labour of love, the journal feels like the afterbirth. It's vital, gives you the space to reflect and seemed to come very quickly after I wrote the initial book!

I'm grateful to my team and clients at Firefly who gave me the encouragement to keep going, particularly Suz Bird my Marketing Director and Lacey Jarrells my VP of Operations. It sometimes feels like we are the three amigos, and they keep me going when my self-doubt kicks in or I'm struggling to focus. Thank you.

To my mentor Patty Aubery for always taking everything to the next level and beyond, pulling me into what I'm capable of, our paths crossed for a reason and I'm eternally grateful.

Significant credit also belongs to the two creative virtuosos who took the vision in my head and made it a reality. Kindah Khalidy created the artwork for the cover for this and Untangled, both of which I love and appreciate more every day. Bhavini Lakhani at B81 Designs worked her design magic to create the pages you have in front of you. Heartfelt thanks to you both.

To my daughter Scarlet for her tolerance of me working on this as she finished her time at school and started university, riding her own waves of change. I love you SB and I really do believe I lucked out to have you as my daughter. I hope you will be able to use some of what's here in these pages to help you face change in your own life.

Lastly to you who have used these pages to reflect and chart a new course. Thank you for trusting me to be your guide. May the materials in this journal help you to move forward with choice and intentionality.

About Kirsty Maynor

Navigating change has been part of Kirsty Maynor's professional and personal life for more than three decades. As a sought-after change strategist, leadership consultant, single mum and someone who has faced divorce, debt, depression and disaster, survivor Kirsty Maynor has traversed some of life's most difficult transitions and emerged happier, smarter and more fulfilled with her resulting career and lifestyle changes.

Kirsty knows what it takes to face a crisis and create better-than-expected outcomes. Now, her simple approach to excelling in the face of change underpins her development work with multinational corporations, executive coaching clients and audiences around the world.

An accomplished coach - certified by the International Coaching Federation with an MSc in organisational behaviour, among numerous other professional credentials - Kirsty is also an award-winning entrepreneur who has dedicated her professional career to helping others live the life of their dreams. The coach to the coaches, she combines years of real-world experiences with advanced study in the field of human potential to coach elite corporate leaders, helping them create futures based on those decisions.

Kirsty is the first Scottish member of the exclusive global Transformational Leadership Council.

Additionally, Kirsty was the first certified facilitator in Scotland of Dr Brené Brown's Dare to Lead™ methodology.

Instagram: kirstymaynor
Facebook: Kirsty Maynor – Author
LinkedIn: Kirsty Maynor
www.kirstymaynor.com

Untangled Journal

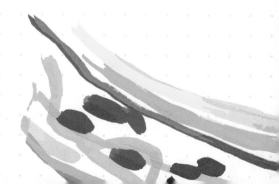